every KID needs Mod PODGe ®

Candice &
Richard Elton

GIBBS SMITH

Gibbs Smith, Publisher
Salt Lake City

First Edition
10 09 08 07 06 5 4 3 2 1

Text © 2006 Candice and Richard Elton
Photographs © Robert Casey
Paper Designs © Dawn DeVries Sokol

Published by
Gibbs Smith, Publisher
P.O. Box 667
Layton, Utah 84041

Orders: 1.800.748.5439
www.gibbs-smith.com

Designed by Dawn DeVries Sokol
Printed and bound in Hong Kong

Disclaimer: Some of the activities suggested in this book require adult supervision. Children and their
guardians should allways use common sense in playing and making crafts. The publisher and authors
assume no responsibility for any damages or injuries incurred while performing any of the activities in this
book, neither are they responsible
for the results of these projects.

Library of Congress Cataloging-in-Publication Data

Elton, Candice.
  Every kid needs mod podge / Candice and Richard Elton ; photographs by
Robert Casey.— 1st ed.
     p. cm.
  ISBN 1-58685-709-6
 1. Decoupage—Juvenile literature. 2. Collage—Juvenile literature. 3.
Glue—Juvenile literature. I. Elton, Richard. II. Title.

TT870.E49 2006
745.54'6—dc22

   2006007988

To our children,
Brigham, Rebekah,
Christian, Sarah,
and Gracee, who
give us inspiration
to keep creating.

cONtEnts

A special thanks to our models
(clockwise from upper left):
Preston Whitney, Morgan Grillone,
Calvin Whitney, Sarah Elton,
Sara Bloom, McKenna Cummins,
and hand-model Rebekah Elton

iNTroDuCtiON

ARE YOU READY TO HAVE SOME CREATIVE KIND OF FUN, to color outside the lines and think outside the box?! Get ready to learn some fresh skills, think of new ideas, and basically go artistically CRAZY by trying something new.

With this book and kit, you can become an artist of "DECOUPAGE"—that's a fancy French word meaning "TO CUT OUT." Decorate your personal items with cutout pieces of colorful paper, magazine clippings, or photographs, and glue them to your "STUFF." You will also become an artist of "COLLAGE"—that's an artistic name for adding many things to a surface and creating your own patterns and style.

By learning to decoupage and make collages, you can put your own artistic stamp on just about anything.

The best decoupage glue—MOD PODGE—will stick your papers to almost any surface and help you create tons of fun projects. When brushed over-top, MOD PODGE adds a glossy shine to your creations.

"MAKE IT YOUR OWN" by covering chipboard with your favorite patterned papers (some are included with the book), add a chain or ribbon, and you have a key chain, zipper pull, bracelet, or necklace.

RUN "WILD" by covering a light switch plate with animal print tissue scraps. Add some decoupage PIZZAZZ to school sup-plies like notebooks and pencils.

FUNK OUT SOME JUNK by making a three-dimensional tin. Design your own piece of wall art. Go to the extreme by decoupaging your tennis shoes, skateboard, or bicycle helmet.

BE MESSY, HAVE FUN, LOOSEN UP . . . SEE WHAT HAPPENS.

What You Get

Brush and wooden stick

2 BOTTLES OF MOD PODGE®

COLLAGE PAPERS made just for you, to cut or tear up and decoupage to your projects.

Six CHIPBOARD shapes, chain and connectors. Add these to your BACKPACKS or make JEWELRY with your own designs.

Light switch plate

Animal print papers to make a "WILD" light covering

Before You StArt

SOME STUFF YOU MAY WANT TO KNOW

MOD PODGE: Decoupage glue can be messy, but remember it's **WASHABLE** and non-toxic.

NEWSPAPER: Put down some before you start your project. You don't want to be decoupaging your mother's dining room table.

YOUR STUFF: Many of these projects use objects from your own stash of stuff. Junk, old tins, boxes, trash, school papers, photos, and notebooks.

CLEAN UP: Use plain old dish soap and water to clean your hands and brushes.

BUYING MORE: You can get more **MOD PODGE** at your local craft store or on the Internet at www.plaidonline.com.

Look for the **ART TIPS** throughout this book to stretch your imagination even further into the world of **MOD PODGE.**

Making it yOUrs

You can **DECOUPAGE** just about anything,
but check with your parents first.

You can use your own artwork from school or wrapping paper
from your last birthday party. The key is to "MAKE IT YOURS"
by using things that you like.

School "DAZE"

Make it yours by using MOD PODGE

on a notebook for school.

ANY
TIM

1 Prepare Surface
Lightly sand the top of your notebook so the MOD PODGE and papers will stick better.

2 Plan Your Design
Look through the papers in the back of this book. When you plan out your design, think like an artist. Move things around. Try different color combinations until you find what you like.

3 Cut or tear out your Papers
Remember, you can use anything you like—papers from this book, old school projects, your own art, notes, wrapping paper, or magazine clippings. There are no rules on this one. And, if you don't like it, you can cover it up or take it off and add something new before it dries.

4 Using MOD PODGE
Pour a small amount onto a paper plate. Use the brush to cover a small part of your notebook with MOD PODGE. Start adding your papers.

LAYERING

To cover the notebook, think in layers.

The background goes first (You're right. It's backwards!)

Then the middle.

Last comes the toppings, your "favorites" like monograms or a special design.

You can MOD PODGE a pencil or pen to match. Just use tiny, leftover scraps.

ART TIP

Notice the color, texture, and design of your project.

5 Push out bubbles
Use the wooden stick to push out any air bubbles. Start in the middle of your paper and gently push to the edge.

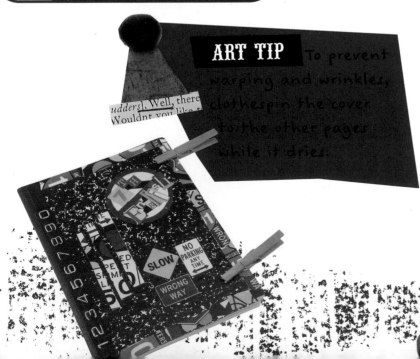

6 Sealing
Once you're finished with your notebook, add one more coat of MOD PODGE over top of everything. This will <u>seal</u> your design. Put it somewhere to dry, and forget about it until the next day.

ART TIP To prevent warping and wrinkles, clothespin the cover to the other pages while it dries.

udders! Well, there Wouldnt you like t

CHIPBOARD Chain

1 Find the chipboard shapes included with this book.

2 Pick out the papers you plan to use for your design.

3 Trace the shape on a piece of paper.

4 Cut it out.

5 Brush the glue on the back of your chipboard.

9 Sand the edges with sandpaper or a nail file to finish.

6 Glue your paper onto the shape.

10 After it dries, poke through the hole with a pencil.

7 Brush glue over the entire shape. This will seal the clipboard.

11 Cut the chain to the desired length with scissors. Put connector on one end of chain. Thread chain through hole. Connect other end of chain to make loop.

8 Let dry.

Hang the shapes on backpacks, pants, keys, or use them for necklaces or bracelets.

DETOUR AHEAD

SPEED LIMIT 50

you rock!

WILD

Light Switch PLATES

Go "wild" with animal prints!

 Lightly sand the light switch plate so that the MOD PODGE will stick.

 Use the animal tissue prints with the book.

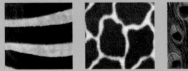 Cut or tear the tissue paper into small pieces.

ART TIP

Make a clean edge by wrapping the paper all the way around the edges.

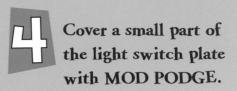 **4** Cover a small part of the light switch plate with MOD PODGE.

5 Put the papers on the light switch plate.

7 Seal the plate by brushing on another coat of MOD PODGE.

6 Keep adding more glue and tissue until you like the way it looks.

8 After it is completely dry, have an adult help you put it on your light switch using screws and a screwdriver. Turn it on and go wild!

WALL Art

COMPOSITION:
THE WAY YOU ARRANGE YOUR STUFF.

1 Dig out that box in your closet (you know the one, the one with all your stuff in it— school papers, ticket stubs, old friendship letters, etc.) and make a piece of wall art.

2 Decoupage your favorite things like magazine clippings, photos, notes, movie or concert tickets, and awards to a piece of poster board or even an old painting that your family doesn't like and thought you tossed away years ago.

3 Use "compostion" to tell a story with your wall art. For example, this piece is arranged to look like a snowboarder on the glistening slopes—we even mixed glitter with the MOD PODGE.

ART TIP

Add words to your designs by cutting up old books, newspapers, comics, magazines, etc. Or select some from the patterned paper in the back of this book. Cut out each letter in the word in a different style, size and color.

Journey TRAVEL BOX

JOURNEY: a trip to one place or another.
TRAVEL: any means of getting there.
BOX: a place to keep your cool things.

...k for the PERFECT BOX by putting ...h your artist eyes. Look around your ...se, in the garage, or maybe you have a favorite junk or treasure box. Here are some we found.

SUR

ART TIP

Something ugly or dirty can be cool if you change it a little. You can change almost anything.

1 Prepare the surface—really go for it this time. Sand it well. Dust off any pieces of wood, paper, or extra junk.

STRESSING

TO MAKE SOMETHING LOOK OLD OR WORN.

You can alter or change the look of your box
and papers by trying these techniques:

1. Wrinkle your paper by scrunching it
up in your hand, then flattening it
back out again.

OR

2. Rip or tear papers unevenly (be
careful not to tear the part of the
picture you like best).

OR

3. Use a stamp inkpad
by rubbing it on the
edge of your paper
or box, this is called
"inking."

OR

4. Add old found
things like papers,
ribbons, buttons, stamps, or alpha-
bet letters. Look for things you can
put in your box, such as collections, tickets, photographs, coins,
or just about anything you've
gathered on your journey.

2 Cut, tear, and layer your
papers. Glue them to the
background first.

3 Glue your found items
to your paper collage.

4 Be sure to seal your project
by brushing MOD PODGE
over top.

domestic arrivals →

JUNK FUNK
3-D

In this project, we'll be doing a 3-D or three-dimensional assemblage. You will be adhering found items to a tin using MOD PODGE.

1 Find a tin with a lid.

2 Get in the drawer and find some junk, like pieces from old games, dominos, coins, buttons, plastic frogs or bugs, stamps, jewelry, dice, checkers, or favorite collections.

3. Decoupage your junk to the tin using the skills you have learned. Since many of the objects will not be flat, glue the largest and flattest area of the object to the tin.

ART TIP

Junk it out by adding an unexpected piece of something— metal washer, candy wrapper, elastic bands, an old earring, etc.

NATURE Journal

ITEMS FROM MOTHER NATURE CAN BE DECOUPAGED TO MAKE A JOURNAL

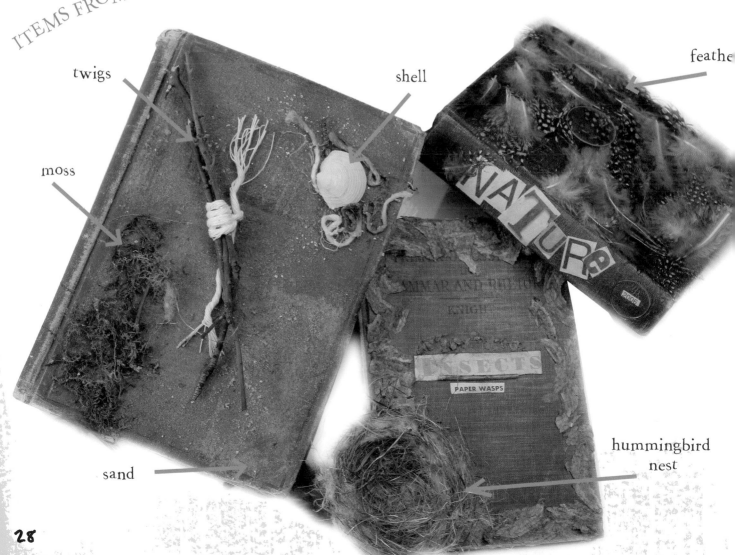

twigs

shell

feathe

moss

NATURE

moss

INSECTS

PAPER WASPS

sand

hummingbird
nest

1 Find a journal or notebook you can use. We used an old book that we could put our nature collections in.

2 Gather some of Nature's gems—things like shells, rocks, wings (butterfly, fairies, or pixies—but be sure to leave the Tooth Fairy alone!), leaves, sand, feathers, etc.

3 Prepare the surface by removing any stickers or labels.

4 Plan your design using your found objects.

5 Use MOD PODGE to glue your objects to your journal. You can use the paper in the back of the book for different backgrounds.

6 Seal your journal, objects and all with one last coat of MOD PODGE.

ADDING TEXTURE:

What is the FEEL of the surface? How ROUGH is it? How SMOOTH?

Using your found objects in your design adds TEXTURE. Try adding some of these items: netting, string, yarn, sand, dirt, and rocks.

ART TIP

Using texture gives you more things to look at and touch.

29

Using PHOTOS

Who doesn't love to look at photos of themselves, their friends, family members and pets? You can add photos to your decoupage projects by using these tricks.

Trick #1:

Get a color or black-and-white copy of your chosen photo on regular white paper.

Trick #2:

Look at your project and think about how big you want your photo to be. Shrink or enlarge your photo on the copier.

ART TIP

Make many copies of the same photo, then you can try different sizes.

Trick #3: Cut around the photo as you wish. You can cut out the person or a shape around the person.

Trick #4: Put MOD PODGE on the back of your photo then stick it to your project.

Trick #5: Make it smooth by pushing down with the side of your wooden stick and squeezing out any bubbles. Be careful not to scratch the photo.

Trick #6: Seal the photo by brushing more MOD PODGE over top when you seal the rest of your project.

ART TIP Add some fun hats, shoes, or even wings to your photos.

EXTREME
Collage

Now that you've learned the basic skills of using
MOD PODGE, you are ready for an EXTREME PROJECT.

These projects are some examples
of kids **GOING TO THE EXTREME.**

Other ideas might include
decoupaging old bedroom furniture
like a nightstand, lamp, or dresser; photo frames;
old books; baseball bat and baseball; or
Frisbee. Use your imagination
BUT MAKE SURE YOU
ASK AN ADULT
FOR
PERMISSION FIRST!

Most of all, CREATE and
HAVE FUN!

The little girl goes out to play

GO 6078

Dude!

Your Specially Designed Decoupage

PATTERNED

RAPErs

5000 LS882796K 日本銀 五千

just be LiVin' Groo

WE'VE GOT SPIRIT! CHARGE! TEAM PLAY BALL!

GO TEAM! SCORE

SLOW

STOP AHEAD

INTERSTATE 101

KEEP → RIGHT WEST

GO

WRONG WAY

ONE WAY

DETOUR AHEAD

STOP

YIELD

SPEED LIMIT 50

NO PARKING ANY TIME

RAIL CROSSING ROAD

REST AREA

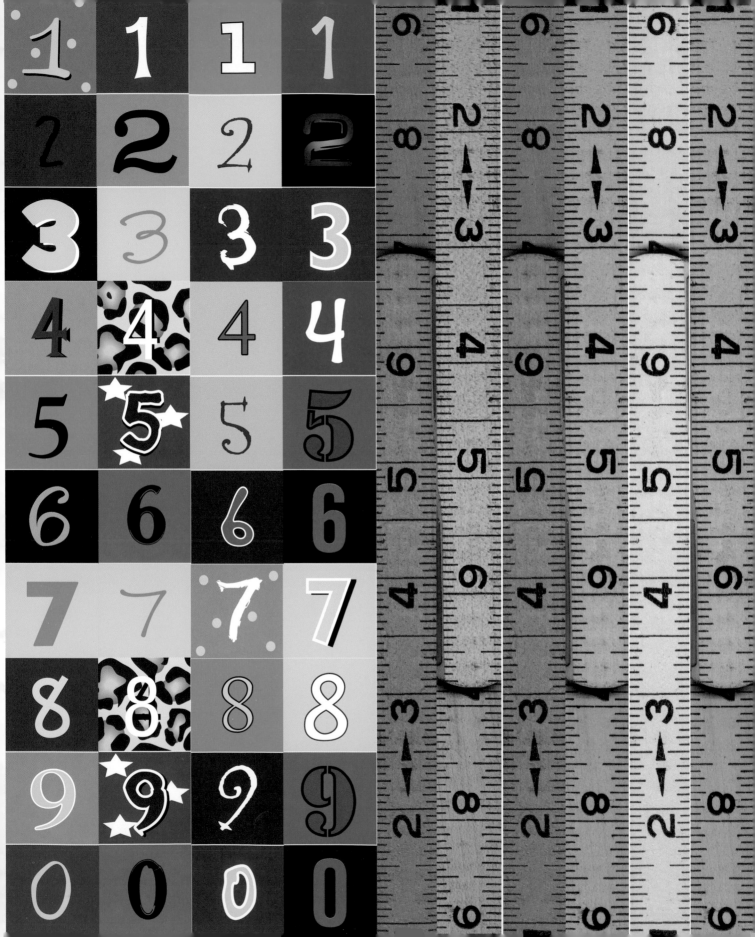

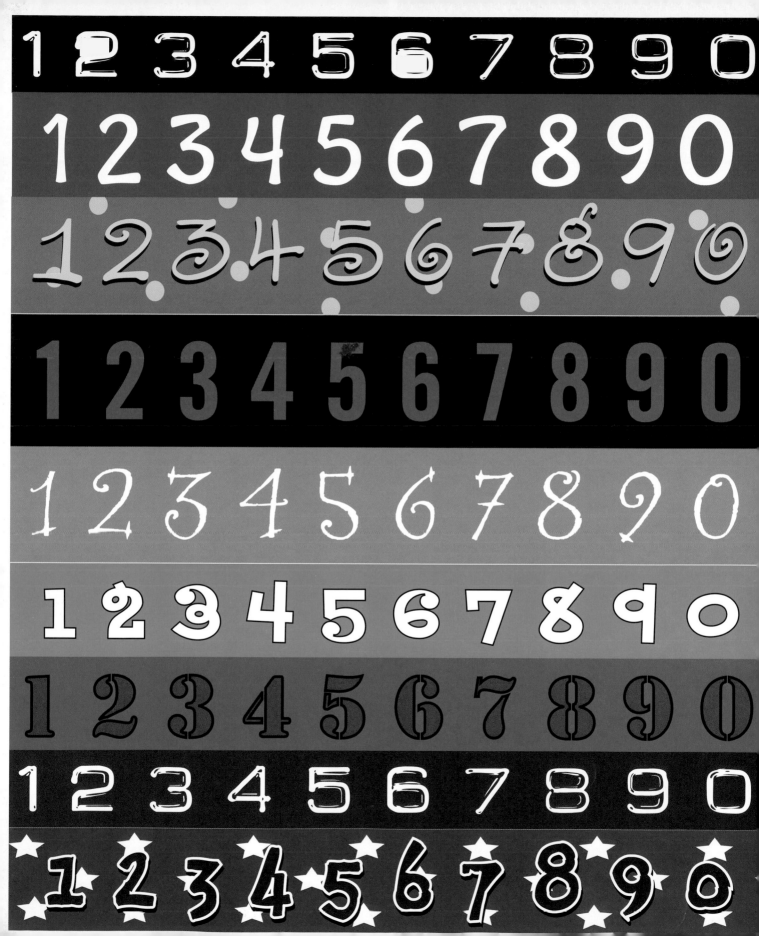

A B C D E F G H I J

K L M N O P Q R

S T U V W X Y Z {} ()

A B C D E F G H I J

K L M N O P Q R

S T U V W X Y Z {} ()

A B C D E F G H I J

K L M N O P Q R

S T U V W X Y Z {} ()

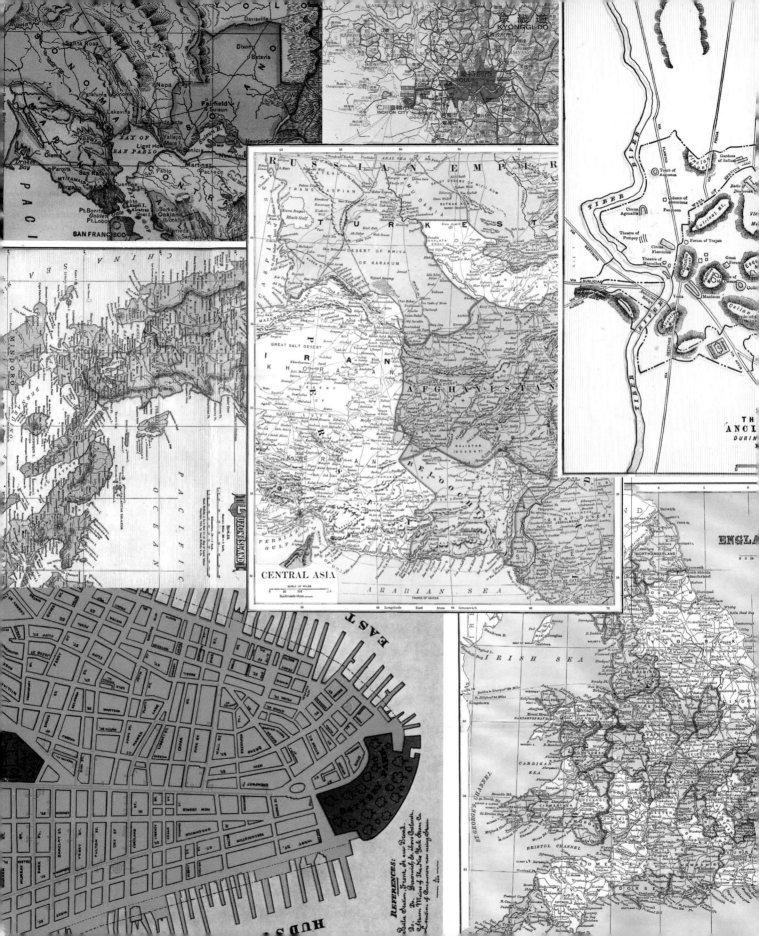

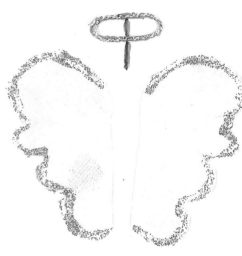